SCHOOL SMART

With Gratitude

Shauna
J.

#BIG   1fins

SCHOOL SMART

It's More Than Just Reading and Writing

SHAUNA F. KING

ISBN: 978-1-4834-6899-0 (sc)
ISBN: 978-1-4834-6898-3 (e)

Library of Congress Control Number: 2017906319

Because of the dynamic nature of the Internet, any web addresses or links contained in this book may have changed since publication and may no longer be valid. The views expressed in this work are solely those of the author and do not necessarily reflect the views of the publisher, and the publisher hereby disclaims any responsibility for them.

Any people depicted in stock imagery provided by Thinkstock are models, and such images are being used for illustrative purposes only. Certain stock imagery © Thinkstock.

Scripture taken from the King James Version of the Bible.

This book is a work of non-fiction. Unless otherwise noted, the author and the publisher make no explicit guarantees as to the accuracy of the information contained in this book and in some cases, names of people and places have been altered to protect their privacy.

Lulu Publishing Services rev. date: 5/26/2017

*This book is dedicated to my parents,
my husband, and my two smart children.*

CONTENTS

Introduction 1

CHAPTER 1 Back to School Blues 5

CHAPTER 2 Off to a Great Start 11

CHAPTER 3 Surviving the First Week 18

CHAPTER 4 Lessons on Discipline 24

CHAPTER 5 Avoiding Power Struggles 30

CHAPTER 6 Tackling the Homework 37

CHAPTER 7 Making the Grade 41

CHAPTER 8 Time for a Conference 47

CHAPTER 9 Handling Spring Fever 52

CHAPTER 10 Keeping Stress in Check 56

CHAPTER 11 Finishing Strong 63

Conclusion 67

INTRODUCTION

Education is the most powerful weapon which
you can use to change the world.
-NELSON MANDELA

"**A**re you ready to go back to school?" I ask my children as the summer ends each year. Their answers range from cheers to groans as thoughts of homework and schedules enter their minds. The excitement or lack thereof is evident in their responses. The truth is, they are not the only ones who feel the joy and apprehension of another school year. As grown-ups, we also feel just as anxious and perplexed when the principal's welcome letter arrives or when retailers blast out their back-to-school commercials.

As an educator, I know the challenges of teaching a class of 35 students. As a mother, I also know the challenges of getting two children to the bus stop on time. I know the demands of preparing student documents for an individual education plan (IEP) meeting, and I know the nervousness of going to a conference for my child's IEP. Both are real challenges that require the adult's full preparation.

As I've traveled the country providing workshops for teachers and parents alike, I have identified common concerns both have throughout the school year: "How do I help my child when I don't understand the homework?" or "How can I keep my students and children motivated?" or "How can I get children and students to follow directions?"

Quite often, these concerns will be addressed in separate books—one for the teachers, one for the parents. This book captures the ebb and flow of a school year in one volume and provides both teachers and parents with effortless strategies that will help children make the most of the nine to ten months they are in school.

As an educational speaker, August is always my busiest month of the year. Professional development for teachers and back-to-school nights for parents are frequent in number and seek to give adults the information they need to help children have a great year. Although these efforts provide a well-meaning foundation, loading up on strategies in one day for a ten-month journey is not the most effective way to ensure student success. From homework, to report cards, to spring fever, to the stress of friendships, school is tough, and not just for the children. We do so much to make sure *they* are ready. We must not forget to make sure *we* are ready for school, as well.

Because I was a teacher before I had children, I remember having quite a few opinions about what parents should do to help their children throughout the school year. Then, I had children of my own, and my son started kindergarten. Every lecture that I'd given parents about "letting your child learn independence and not peeking into the classroom" went out the window. It was different when it was *my* child. Now, as both parent and educator, my perspectives have grown. Raising and teaching children is such hard work, yet it is a truly rewarding experience. The assortment of emotions that children can bring is like none other. You can truly love them with your whole heart, and in the next moment, wonder why you chose to have or work with children. There are delightful moments when you feel that your cup *runneth* over, and then there are other moments when you want to run away and put yourself in a timeout.

I wrote this book to support anyone who supports children, in the school house or your own house. For our children to be successful, we have to do just as much throughout the year to prepare and sustain ourselves as we ask our children to. As each year passes, our children are learning more, growing more, and developing more expectations of themselves and us. The chapters of this book flow through the course of the school year and provide guidance that doesn't require a postgraduate education degree or a six-week parenting course (as most of us don't have time for either). As you read this book, my hope is that you understand that each school year is a journey through which we have the privilege of coaching our children to make smart choices. Teachers and parents have different roles, yet both are steering toward the same destination. If we think of school as a sports game, then the child is the star player and we are the coaches on the sidelines, guiding and cheering them as they fumble, score, and pass.

School is a huge part of a child's journey to adulthood. Our job as adults is to model and teach children that smart is not just something you are, but something you become. Each year, children gain new knowledge and skills and learn to make smart decisions and, with any luck, so do we. Enjoy the journey.

CHAPTER 1

Back to School Blues

Every new beginning comes from some other beginning's end.
-SENECA

There's a prominent shift of energy that tends to happen somewhere around the third week of August. It's not a seasonal shift because the weather is still hot and muggy. It's not a shift to prepare for a holiday because Labor Day is still weeks away. The shift that occurs will last through the fall, winter, and spring and affects hundreds of thousands of children and their parents. The shift that I'm speaking of is the "back-to-school" shift.

As major retailers begin to push the latest trends in backpacks and children's fashion, children, parents, and educators begin to feel the pressure of the back-to-school rush. From physicals and late registration to long trips to the mall, the growing anticipation of returning to a structured learning environment becomes imminent.

Though we're all aware that school must start again, it still catches us by surprise and causes a variety of emotions to swell within us. For our children, the idea of decreased playtime and increased homework time, hours in a classroom setting, and structure brings on an unsettling feeling. To them, the beginning of school is the end of freedom and jubilant times. Sure, they'll have breaks and weekends to regroup and enjoy at their leisure. However, until that last day of school, however, those small breaks are like dangling a carrot in front of a horse. There's the promise of a great reward, but they've got to be urged to keep moving.

For a parent, the end of summer break means the beginning of a "tug-and-pull" relationship with your child. As a parent, you'll begin the constant discussions of schoolwork, alarm clocks, bus schedules, projects, picking out clothes for school, extracurricular activities, field trips, and general school routines. These conversations won't be easy, and they won't always work out in your favor. They are, however, as much a part of the education process as homework and testing. So, you can expect the tug-of-war with your child to continue from August until June of each year, with small breaks in between.

For an educator, the back-to-school season is filled with preparation—mentally, emotionally, and academically. As a teacher or administrator, you're going to be focused entirely on building your classroom environment and assignments that help meet qualitative and quantitative goals. Objectives need to be met and standards need to be set. Last year's performance is either an indicator of what to expect in the current school year or a guide to what not to do this year. Mentally and emotionally, the idea of taking on fifteen or more students and their fifteen ever-evolving personalities can be enough to keep you up at night or make you consider a career outside the classroom. For you, the back-to-school shift means proving that learning and hard work is important and worth the ongoing challenges that may be ahead.

One way for any of these groups to master the back-to-school shift is to look at it as an obstacle course, in which each hurdle, ditch, and groove are meant to build your tenacity and bring you closer to the finish line. The educational obstacle course never starts off easy. In fact, the course starts way before the whistle blows or the flag is waved. It starts the moment a child responds to a nursery rhyme, babbles his or her way through a sentence, or excitedly responds to a picture book. From those tender moments, the educational obstacle course begins to develop its path. The pace changes—anxiously urging a child to learn faster and sometimes ahead of his or her current intellectual capacity. If, however, everyone involved in the educational process remembers the end goal is to help students develop to their best potential and perform at their highest peaks, the obstacle course gets easier to navigate. If everyone can master the back-to-school mindset and look at it as a groove in the educational obstacle course, then we can increase our stamina and our patience, endure the course, and come out victorious.

We must do certain things to prepare for the annual shift that happens during August. And as routine as shopping for school supplies, organizing school uniforms and clothes, or remembering bus schedules can be, this is a fraction of the preparation needed to fully grasp what *back to school* really entails.

First, we must focus on the child. Regardless, whether we're the parent or the educator, our primary concern and connection is the student. During the final weeks before school starts, it's important to remember the goal is to tap into each student's intellectual and artistic curiosities and motivate them to learn more. They should be interested in learning more about themselves, the world we live in and the requisite skills to function and become successful in the world. We can sum that up as reading, writing, and arithmetic, but we know all too well there's so much more to learn than these subjects.

When we focus on children, we understand that their minds are bottomless and their imaginations are endless. We can fill them with information, yet they'll be more curious, intrigued, and plagued with comments. Therefore, we should make every honest and intentional effort to quench their curiosities. We must focus on building lesson plans that engage their five senses and enhance their perspectives of learning. We must utilize all of our time for instruction and relationship building while striving to meet and exceed benchmarks. We must pull students from the rear, and at a minimum, push them toward the center of our attention so that, eventually, they can be at the head of the class. We must use positive talk that's honest, encouraging, hopeful, and strategic. At all times, we must put students first with what and how we teach them. We must have a strong and consistent desire to meet students where they are and elevate their experiences. When we do this, students become lifelong learners—inside and outside of the classroom. The world becomes their oyster.

Preparation has so much to do with giving and receiving a proper education. Therefore, the final few weeks before school starts, parents and educators should spend a significant amount of time preparing for a child's learning experience. Everything from organizing classrooms and bedrooms, scheduling before- and after-school activities to picking school supplies and accessories should be well thought-out and strategic. The goal is to create a 360-degree approach to giving and receiving information, where it starts with the adults, passes to the children and benefits society.

You, the adult in charge of a child's learning experience, should do three core things to properly prepare for the school year. First, prepare your patience. The school year has start and end dates but will be a continuous pull on your energy, time, confidence, and most definitely, your patience. Children, whether they're in primary or secondary education levels, require a special kind of patience. They require the type of patience that understands they are still children. Children are innocent, fearful, and immature yet can show laziness, moodiness, and extreme drama.

Developing this type of patience is a process. Don't expect it to appear at a moment's notice or to increase in extremely demanding situations. Instead, begin to work on it weeks before school starts with the hopes it doesn't have to be tested on the very first day of school.

Second, prepare your strategy. In terms of educating and dealing with children, strategy goes beyond schedules and lesson plans. You should develop strategies for teaching, correcting, and reinforcing expectations. These strategies should address poor performance, surprising accomplishments, social advancements, emotional pitfalls, engagement, and isolation. The list goes on and on. Your strategy to deal with complex situations could help you manage all the emotional and mental strains you'll encounter during the school year. Be smart, and be prepared with a strategy. Take time to develop a comprehensive list of ways you'll celebrate, teach or correct a child, as the strategy you use in some situations could have long-term effects on his or her psychological and emotional development. So be prepared, well in advance, with necessary strategies to ensure your students are fully aware of the moments they're doing great as well as those moments when they could do better.

Third, prepare to ask some hard questions. How will this school year be different? What will everyone learn? How will everyone grow? What kind of relationships will the students form with others; will they understand that relationships come and go? Will everyone be safe? These are just a few of the questions that'll be on our minds until the day before school starts. What makes these questions easier to address and evaluate, is how much we prepare ourselves and each other as we make the transition from summer break to a new school year.

CHAPTER 2

Off to a Great Start

The secret of getting ahead is getting started.
- MARK TWAIN

As the sun begins to rise and mark the first day of a new school year, parents, teachers, and students are filled with a range of emotions and fueled by the bustling activities of getting off to school. Some of us awaken with surging adrenaline, ready to conquer the day and make a great first impression. Others awaken full of nerves and uncertainty about the days ahead.

Although we have different roles to fill as parents, teachers, and students, we all are connected by a common fiber: we must spend the next few months entirely focused on becoming the best we can be. Of course, children hold the bulk of this responsibility, but they can't do it without us. Therefore, the first day of school sets the tone for our purpose, which is to educate students so wholesomely that it positively affects the rest of their lives.

Ironically, on the first day of school, our children's education is probably the last thing on our minds. Sure, we're sending them off to school, expecting them to return home a tad smarter than before they left. We're more concerned, however, with how they're adjusting to new teachers, a new schedule, new classmates—who are just as anxious as they are—and the typical chaos that comes with the first day of school. Ideally, we'd wake up our children, get them dressed, give them their lunches, send them off to school, and have no issues or concerns until they arrive home. What actually happens on this monumental day is far from that ideal.

As teachers, we sometimes question whether we've prepared enough. Did we have ample time to review our curriculum and prepare our materials? Are we prepared for potential class dynamics as each student's individual needs and personality enter the room? Are our classrooms organized and designed to help the students function, engage with their learning experiences, learn independently, and access information quickly? Have students been properly prepared for the concepts we have to teach? Will the students understand how we grade them, what they're expected to learn, how this information will improve their education in addition to our policies for things like behavior, attitude, and performance? Most importantly, we'll question our ability to get the job done. We'll have questions about whether or not we have what it takes to meet the standards of the school, the district, and the state. If we add in variables such as new colleagues, new administrators, tighter budgets, and schedules, or changing grade levels and schools, the first day of school can make us feel just as anxious and emotionally overwhelmed as our students.

The key to navigating the first day of school, from a teacher's perspective, is confidence. We typically tell our students that they need to rely on their confidence to conquer the school day, but teachers also must remind themselves about confidence. For a leader, confidence is an imperative, especially on a day as important as the first day of school. Demonstrating insecurity or uncertainty does not help to create the safe learning environment that you want to provide for your students. Children appreciate a teacher who commands the respect and the attention of the class. Show them you are the adult by demonstrating poise, confidence, and leadership.

As a teacher, before you head out of the door on the first day of school, check your confidence. Dig deep to establish trust within yourself. If you've been serious and diligent about preparing for a phenomenal school year, then there's no need to feel inferior or underqualified. Silence your inner critic! If your negative chatter becomes audible, you'll lose your composure and you'll struggle with looking, feeling, and sounding confident. When you reach the school building, approach it with the self-assurance that your job is necessary, you're appreciated, and what you're doing for the students will make an impact on the rest of their lives. Your role in society is critical. The mere fact that you chose an honorable yet underappreciated career of being an educator proves that you are a confident leader with the ability to influence change.

From a parent's perspective, the first day of school is a time of relief and grief. Finally! The kids are out of the house! No more expensive, yet underwhelming, summer camps. No more refrigerator raids. No more taunting chants of "I'm bored." As parents, we love our children and enjoy quality time with them, but the summer break can be mentally exhausting. Watching children head off to school for the first time in months, however, can tug at our heartstrings for a number of reasons.

First, as parents, we're concerned about our children. Our concern ranges from their safety, relationships, and experiences, to their preparation and happiness. During their time away from us, we often worry about them because we're not there to protect them. Our vision from those "eyes in the back of our head" is blurred. The ability to overhear the conversations that could get them in trouble is muted. We're not there to cushion their falls, remind them to stay focused, or immediately reprimand them when they do wrong. The school puts us as the secondary point of contact because whatever our children do goes through other channels before it reaches us. And that alone is enough to cause concern.

Second, we're slightly self-conscious. The summer slide is a reflection of what we've done with our children during their break from school. Suddenly, on the first day of school, we think about all the times we let them play video games longer than we should have. Or all the times that we overlooked their midnight bedtimes and starting the day at noon. We think about how those summer packets weren't even touched until a few days before school started. And all of those instances make us extremely nervous about how they'll perform during the school year.

Finally, we're overwhelmed. *Their* tighter schedules mean *we* have tighter schedules. We can't go to bed or wake up later because our children can't do it, either. Their deadlines become our deadlines. All their papers, projects, assignments, and reminders become encircled on our personal calendars and constantly remind us of the extra work we have to do. Their educational experiences become our educational experiences. When they do well, we feel good. When they perform badly, we feel awful. Although we're not the ones in school for several hours each day, we become sympathetic parents who endure the same experiences as our children. We, however, pile those experiences on top of our own experiences, duties, and responsibilities.

Navigating the first day of school as a parent means finding a way to balance everything. We have to balance their responsibilities with our own. We have to manage our emotions so that they don't trickle down to our children.

Approach the first day of school with optimism. It's a new beginning and a fresh start for you and your child. Even if the last school year wasn't as promising as you'd hoped, or the summer break was less structured than you would have liked, the new school year is a chance to correct everything. If you approach the first day of school as if it were an opportunity to do better and pick up where you left off, then each day throughout the school year is like opening a new door and a chance to make a new start. You can aggressively deal with challenges as you progress toward your next goal.

For students, the first day of school is a roller coaster. They want to show off how they've physically changed over the summer or their new gear, but they don't yet want to deal with the structure and obligations of school. They want to reconnect with their friends, but they don't want to be limited with their social time. They want to get the school year over with, but they don't want it to start. Of course, all students are different and their age and perception of the school will play a strong part in the experiences they have. The one constant, however, is that the first day of school will evoke a variety of emotions.

Students don't necessarily focus on how much they're learning as much as they focus on the assignments that they're expected to complete. They don't focus on the classroom's design as much as they focus on the feeling the classroom gives them. They don't focus on the qualifications and preparation of the teacher as much as they focus on whether or not they actually like their teacher's personality or appearance. For students, the first day of school is a "feeling" more than an occasion.

Although we may not clearly remember what we felt like when we were their age, the truth is, we're not in their shoes. We don't know what they *should* be feeling because we aren't them. We've had the fortunate experience of growing up and maturing, which ironically, minimizes a lot of our youthful emotional connections. It's challenging to connect to our six-year-olds and honestly say that we know what they're feeling like because those feelings have been replaced. We can't quite connect to our teenager's emotions, although we once were teens, because those emotions have been replaced, too. Growing up definitely gives us the right to say, "been there and done that," but honestly, we may not clearly remember how we felt during those times. We just remember what we learned from the experiences. Our childhood feelings have been replaced with lessons learned.

On the first day of school, help your child deal with his or her emotions by reinforcing that this day is a part of the process of growing up. Everything that they do and feel on the first day of school is a part of getting older, smarter, and more prepared for the future. If they feel nervous, reinforce that they'll be okay.

Listen to them and ask about their apprehensions, and address them with positive talk and optimism. They need to feel secure. If they feel excited, reinforce their excitement by increasing yours. Don't meet their excitement with concern. Allow students to feel the adrenaline and let it drive their day. If they feel angry, reinforce their memories of happier times. Allow them to voice their frustrations and give them ideas about how they can constructively eliminate their anger.

In reality, it's the first day of school for parents, teachers, and children. We'll all have different stories, feelings, and thoughts. The playing field has been leveled for all of us, so no one has a greater advantage over another. If we keep that in mind, we can help each other get through this day. And depending on how committed we are to reaching goals and milestones, we also can help each other get through the year.

CHAPTER 3

Surviving the First Week

Motivation is what gets you started.
Habit is what keeps you going.

- JIM RYUN

Surviving the first day of school is half of the battle. So, once you've been able to handle that day, the first week of school should get easier. The first week is filled with a ton of experiences that begin to shape what is to come throughout the school year. With the understanding that just a few days may define how we adjust to life for the next nine months, it's super important to ensure that these first few days are the most structured and enjoyable days for parents, teachers, and students.

Within the first days, relationships have formed or broken, expectations have been set, habits have formed, and everyone generally knows the routine. The scheduling kinks have been worked out, which means that everyone knows where they should be at designated times. This alleviates so much stress and many feelings of being overwhelmed. Scheduling, especially during the first week of school, is one of the major things that can severely affect everyone's perception of how smoothly the school year will go.

Your child has reconnected and disconnected with some of his or her peers, which means the bumpiest parts of the emotional rollercoaster have passed. Often, the summer break provides opportunities for your child to build new relationships, understand more about themselves, and recognize the traits or qualities that they're looking for in friends. Simple things like what their friends talk about, how they behave, what they wear, and who their new friends are, will affect how your child responds to both new and old friends.

In addition to child-to-child relationships, teachers have formed new relationships as well. They have a general idea about the students with whom they will be able to communicate easily. They know which colleagues to turn to for help, a listening ear, support, and friendship. They also know which parents may be extremely involved and which ones will be hardly available. Teachers will oversee the relationships with their students and have a strong indication of who to pair and separate based on performance, social engagement, and education concerns.

Parents also will form relationships. In fact, the relationships in which parents are involved will be some of the longest standing relationships throughout the school year. As a parent, we're evaluating everyone. We form relationships with teachers based on our perception of their competence and ability to provide guidance for our children. If the teacher shows a strong skill in educating, inspiring, and motivating our children, then our relationships with the teachers will be more trusting and supportive. If the teacher shows signs of being ill-prepared, our relationships may be strained and critical. If administrators communicate well and demonstrate competence, we are excited to partner with them as they lead our children's school. Conversely, if the administrators are regularly unavailable and appear disengaged, we are less patient and supportive of them. Finally, we evaluate our children's friends. If they are just as excited and driven as our children, then we encourage relationships between them. If, however, they don't show signs of meeting the challenges of the school year or helping our children become better people, then we try to discourage the relationship before it really has a chance to form.

Along with the scheduling and relationships that form during the first week of school, expectations begin to settle in. Although it sounds cliché, take each day one at a time. Create a checklist of goals you would like to accomplish during this first week. A checklist will allow you to focus on small significant steps that help you to finish the first week feeling very accomplished and ready to tackle the next phase. Some of us are up for the challenge. Some of us need constant encouragement to make it through each day. And some of us are looking for the nearest exit, with the hopes that we can buy just a little more time before things become so serious. Either way, the first week of school lets everyone know where they stand, where they need to be headed, and exactly how they're going to get there.

Now, just because we know the route to finishing the school year's educational journey, it doesn't make it an easy trip. At several points along the way, especially during the first week of school, the road ahead will seem long and daunting. It will take much fortitude and an earnest desire to excel in meeting the expectations that lie ahead. We'll pull on every fiber in our brains and bodies to stay committed to the task at hand—properly and successfully educating our children. However, if within the first week of school, we can manage to look at the route toward the finish line, figure out our pit stops, refuel with positive experiences, and become strategic about the last few laps, then the road to the end of the school year will become more manageable and even exciting.

To fully embrace the first week of school and make the best of it, every person involved in a child's education, including the child, should look at each day like a task on a checklist. Perhaps, by assigning one goal to each day, we can finish the first week feeling accomplished and ready to tackle the next phase.

For example, on day one, if everyone focuses on building relationships, then we'll all feel much better at the end of the day when we've met new people, reconnected with friends, and figured out what we have in common with others. Teachers should try to learn the names of all of their students. Incorporate "getting to know you" activities to build a positive classroom community. At the onset of day one, we'll know what we want or expect from that day. So, any mishaps we encounter will be trivial while we're in pursuit of getting acquainted with one another.

Day two may be focused on adjusting to a new schedule. Everyone could pay attention to time management by working out the challenges of bus schedules, class schedules, and work schedules. We can adjust our alarms and reminders; update our calendars with important events; synchronize our work, school, and extracurricular activities; and generally, identify when and where we're supposed to be.

Day three could focus on getting familiar with the different expectations that each teacher has. From how to head papers, to how to organize binders, each teacher will have different rules and preferences. Focusing on how to meet those expectations and come to each class fully prepared can reduce feelings of being overwhelmed and prevent decreases in points and grades because of inattentiveness to a teacher's preferences.

Day four could be focused on filling in the blanks with supplies. We know the routine: parents get a generic school supply list before school starts, but teachers have a custom list requesting different things. So, perhaps we could focus on finalizing the school supply run, organizing the supplies, and ensuring that everyone has what they need. This little task of stocking up, especially while things are on sale, actually may prevent a lot of the "I ran out of supplies" groans we hear from children throughout the school year.

Finally, day five could be focused on communication. It may not seem smart to put communication as the last item on this list, but everyone should take the first four days to make observations and notes. Now, the adults can ask meaningful questions and have more purposeful conversations. A lot of information is covered within the first few days of school. So, before you jump to conclusions or feel overwhelmed, take the time to observe and wait for information to be shared. If after the first few days, your questions still haven't been answered or your concerns haven't been addressed, using the last day of the first week of school to get everything clarified displays maturity, patience, and keen observation skills.

By treating the first week of school like a goal sheet, we can proudly mark off our completed tasks, surging feelings of accomplishment, competence, intelligence, and hope. Parent, teachers, and students can build a goal sheet for the first week of school according to your own preferences and needs. Remember to relax. You will make it through this first week and then you will be more confident to make it through the remainder of the year.

CHAPTER 4

Lessons on Discipline

Intellect plus character; that is the goal of true education.
– DR. MARTIN LUTHER KING, JR.

The word *discipline* comes from the Latin *disciplina*, meaning "teaching, learning." Throughout the year, adults are responsible for providing discipline and teaching children how to operate in school. We want children to understand how focus and hard work go hand in hand throughout their educational journey, but ultimately, we also want them to understand that focus leads to better results. Sometimes, when we want children to focus, we have to be a little firmer and stricter than we'd otherwise like to be. The idea of "tough love" seems to be a prominent characteristic that helps children understand the concept of focus and discipline. Some teachers, however, have developed a different kind of approach to showing students that they want what's best for them.

As a new teacher, I was handed a piece of advice that I'll

always remember: don't smile before Christmas. Although the phrase seems to make a recommendation that teachers shouldn't be kind or gentle, it's actually geared less toward personality and more toward performance. The "don't smile before Christmas" adage reminds teachers that the fragile period between the first day of school and the day before winter break should be centered on building expectations and building relationships. This is all a part of the discipline or teaching process.

Making students familiar with class procedures, requirements, and expectations will ultimately hold them accountable for their performance. They develop a higher level of self-respect, integrity, and responsibility for their learning. "Don't smile before Christmas" is a gentle push to teach students how to understand their roles within their educational experiences.

Now, a lack of "smiling" does not mean a lack of friendliness or display of respect and approachability. Children learn best through positive relationships that set high expectations while also making them feel safe, secure, and nurtured. All teachers should do their best to make both students and their parents feel welcomed, cared for, and appreciated.

Teachers are expected to set the pace and the long-term goals for their students. This is why curricula are well planned, progress is monitored, and tests are given. Educators are tasked with the responsibility of making sure that every student who sets foot in a formal learning environment is well equipped with the tools and information they'll need to succeed. Therefore, it is imperative that we stand behind any method or adage that puts the student's education first. Our students approach our classrooms with various background issues relating to their home environments, social relationships, and, of course, hormonal development. This often means that teachers aren't getting students at their best and have to manage those issues in addition to managing the educational experience.

This huge responsibility also means that teachers have to prioritize agendas when it comes to giving students exactly what they need. And, in most cases, what they need most is information, tools, and resources that help them to succeed in life and in school.

Parents have a lot of responsibility on their plates. Raising children, working, running a household, and providing a safe and nurturing environment is enough to consume a 24-hour day. In addition to those requirements, parents also are tasked with sending their children to school in their "right minds" and prepared to focus on their education. Children come to school with a wide range of emotions from anger to tiredness to hopelessness and anxiety. These issues are tucked into backpacks along with incomplete homework and unsigned notices and carried to school for the teacher to deal with while delivering the lesson.

Gone are the days in which the teacher is only required to teach and provide academic support. In 21st-century schools many teachers, especially the high-performing ones, take on the responsibility of giving out hugs, talking about the personal challenges of their students, and filling in the emotional gaps as needed. This type of teacher-student relationship, which focuses on the wholeness of a child's learning experience, may benefit the child but can be taxing on the teacher if he or she is unprepared for the task.

Therefore, parents must stay connected with the social and

emotional needs of their children. This means talking with your children and listening to them. It requires using positive talk to reduce anxieties and concerns. Parents should go through backpacks and review notebooks with their children, making sure that they are as up to date as their children are concerning their schoolwork and communication with the teacher. Parents should address their grievances, cheer for their accomplishments, and do everything necessary to send their children to school with one focus: to get the best educational experience they can possibly get.

Children also play a significant role in enhancing this needed focus and discipline. It's so easy for them to shift the blame of missed assignments on parents who were "too busy" and teachers who "didn't tell us what to do." They'll also shift the blame on their struggles with work claiming that it was "too hard" or friends were "too distracting." The point is that children rarely take responsibility for their actions or the inevitable consequences. This is why it's important that we, as parents and teachers, instill a foundation of focus, discipline, and, most important, accountability in children.

Children are constantly watching the consistency or inconsistency of the adults in their lives. Sometimes, as adults, we allow them the room to get out of things we don't deem to be "important," but this can lead to a habit of allowing children to escape responsibility. We have to be consistent and teach them that their roles have responsibilities, and whether or not those responsibilities are fun, they still must be met. Focus and discipline make their lives better. It may be "uncool" or too time-consuming, but if they want to become the best they can be, create work they can be proud of, and enjoy a lifetime of rewards, focus and discipline lay the path toward achieving those results.

Therefore, as children grow they should be tasked with adjusting how they think about the role they play in relation to their education. They must do their part to show up prepared, and if they are unprepared, they must do their part to get prepared, do their part of learning, and if learning becomes difficult, ask questions. They must learn to focus and practice discipline, and if focusing becomes difficult, do their part to limit distractions. As parents and teachers, we are to provide guidance and support as children adjust to their ever-developing roles.

This is the point: we all have jobs to do along this educational journey. And just like regular 9-to-5 jobs, these jobs have expectations and requirements. Additionally, just like other jobs, there's a probationary period. For the sake of this chapter, the period between the first day of school and the last day before winter break is the probationary period for the student, parent, and the teacher.

During a regular probationary period, you are required to show your understanding and acceptance of the tasks you're assigned, in addition to demonstrating your ability to collaborate, engage, work independently, and strive for excellence. This is exactly the foundation that should be set for the educational experience at all times, and most especially during this probationary period. If all of us, the parents, students, and teachers, treat our role in the education experience as jobs, in which we are expected to perform our best with the prospect of achieving consistent rewards, we can meet our goals. We can agree that the students are our first priority, so we must do everything possible to ensure that they receive a quality learning experience. And if we do this long enough with enough precision and determination, we can all smile before Christmas and throughout the year.

CHAPTER 5

Don't Take the Bait: Avoiding Power Struggles

One of the best gifts adults can give children
is the gift of a good example.
-SHAUNA KING

Whether it's the first day of school or the end of the first month, it's inevitable. Children will test the limits of their power with any of the adults with whom they interact. Whether it's a verbal combat, attitudinal altercation, or an unfortunate physical encounter, as children try to figure out who they are, they also try to figure out how much power they have.

We see this in the classroom when it comes to daily communication, dealing with projects and assignments, or routine classroom participation. As teachers, we never know what emotional baggage our students are bringing to the table. Therefore, we never really know which end of the tug-of-war rope we're going to be pulling. As parents, you'll deal with their hormonal growth, which can put your child on an emotional rollercoaster filled with spiral, loops, and bumpy rides. No matter what our adult roles are, children will test the rules and restrictions placed on them—simply because that's what all children do as they navigate their way from childhood to adolescence to adulthood.

We first encounter a child's need for autonomy and control during his or her early childhood years. Parents and teachers hear everything from "I can do it by myself" to insatiable questions that start with "Why?" Often in these moments, children are trying to test authority, exhibit their inquisitiveness, and, ultimately, find their own path. The trick, however, is for us to determine how to balance a child's quest for independence and autonomy with our knowledge and maturity.

Isn't it humbling that we find ourselves debating with people more than 20 years our junior, and often lose that battle? Of course, we try to outsmart them and we try to exhort our power over them, but any wise adult knows that we often lose the power struggle and, ultimately, reveal how powerless we can be. The truth is that we really can't make anyone do anything and this includes children. I'm sure you're saying, "Oh, yes I can." But really think about it, are you *making* anyone do something or providing an environment in which they choose to do what you have requested? If we could make others do what we want, many adults would make everyone in our path do exactly as we desired. And this not only includes children or students but also includes spouses and the slow drivers blocking traffic. As adults, it's important to realize a couple of things. First, we need to understand that children are growing and curious beings and we shouldn't take their behavior personally. Second, we have to use their quest for control over their own decisions and their responsibilities as opportunities to teach them patience, negotiation, and respect.

In the so-called "good old days," children were taught to mind their manners and their business, which ultimately led to the "do as I say, not as I do" model of enforcing obedience. Sure, it was probably much easier to keep children obedient and easier to manage their behavior when they had "no right" to question the instructions of any adult. As these "obedient" children began to get a taste of their independence, however, they often also felt the need to rebel against every "no," "don't do that," and "because I said so!" they'd ever heard.

Power struggles seem to begin when one party doesn't want to let go of the control they have over another party or a shared situation. Often, when it comes to a child's education, the adults (teachers, administrators, and parents) have all the control, whereas the children simply are left with taking orders and delivering results. Any person who is put in a situation in which they constantly are expected to be submissive or agreeable naturally will feel the need to lash out or regain some sort of control—even if it's just enough control to soothe a bruised ego. That being said, power should never be a struggle because both sides should have rights, privileges, autonomy, and responsibilities that allow them to contribute authority and accept authority.

Remember, when it comes to a child's education, our ultimate goal is to provide skills and information that he or she will retain and access in their personal and professional lives, and value for the rest of his or her life. This means that from the very beginning, as parents and teachers, we adults have to learn strategies that reduce the pain and increase the potential of our children.

There is one mindset shift that I've come to learn should be embraced when it comes to handling children's behavior. It has the acronym QTIP, which stands for *Quit Taking It Personally.* As adults, we often take it personally when a child responds in a way that we find disrespectful. Whether we like to admit it or not, a feeling of anger or loss of control often arises as we try to convince our students or children to follow our direction the first time. I recall one of my middle-school students asking me "Why do I have move?" when I asked him to change seats after he was constantly talking to his neighbor. My mind screamed, "Because I said so! And how dare you not do what I asked?" I was immediately irritated and frustrated with this student's question and my emotional pressure gauge skyrocketed. My response was largely due to the adult-size ego that comes with the adult-size responsibility placed on us to rear and teach respectful, appreciative, and intelligent children.

Often, a behavior is a child's way of telling you that some need is not being met. If we QTIP and learn not to take groans, occasional outbursts, and immature behavior as an affront, we can tap into the "bigger picture" behind these responses to us and respond to them effectively.

Whether social, emotional, or physical, these needs cause children, who haven't yet learned how to rationalize, compartmentalize, or otherwise make sense of their situation, to engage in power struggles with authority figures. What they're doing is trying to gain some type of ground on which to stand to avoid feeling like they have no control whatsoever over their lives and feelings. We, as parents and educators, take this very personally.

Children are often reactive and more outspoken than we are. It may be due to their underdeveloped prefrontal cortex that controls their impulses. They speak what's in their minds and hearts because they haven't yet developed the executive function skill of filtering their thoughts, feelings, and communication. Some would argue that it would be great if we could walk around expressing exactly how we felt without a filter or consideration about how the other person might take it. But that's not the real world and maturity and tact definitely play a major role in how far we go in our lives. Because children haven't matured sufficiently to understand the dynamics of the world we live in, they bait us with their questions, emotional outbursts, and rants. On top of that, they continue to pout or sometimes even listen to us as we explain the importance of what we're asking them to do. For them, behavior is simply a part of finding their power. For us, this is a part of our job as adults.

What we should learn about power struggles is that this type of emotional, social, and mental development is not only appropriate, it's also kind of necessary. Think about it: how do we learn to grow, make mistakes, and bounce back if we don't, at first, question the situations we're in and how we can get out of them. We have to remember that we, too, once were children who questioned everything (even if only in our heads) and often wanted to have answers before we participated in the requests of others. In fact, we kind of do that now as adults. We've just learned how to go with the flow and pick our battles.

To handle power struggles the smart way, learn to be

intentional about trying always to model calmness, confidence, and concern. Learn which behaviors trigger a negative response from you. Practice what you teach and model how you would want the child to respond when challenged or disrespected. Plan how you will respond the next time the child misbehaves. It is easier to change a child's behavior by changing your behavior first. If parents react negatively to "bait statements," such as "why do I have to do my homework now?" or if teachers respond to "you're not my mom," it teaches children that we can easily be triggered and lose control. As a self-proclaimed "Yelling Teacher in Recovery," I learned this lesson the hard way. Often, I would lose my cool with students and my children and unintentionally reinforce negative behavior. Think of your plan well before the potential battle begins. Will you be intentional about taking a breath before you respond or will you immediately respond with, "Homework must be done before the TV is turned on"? Will you calmly and non-sarcastically respond with "You're right, I'm not your mom, but I care very much about you," or "You're right, I'm not your mom, so I think we should give her a call to discuss what just happened"? The funny thing about power struggles is that you can demonstrate your power by being calm and confident and not losing your cool. And I can tell you, from experience as an educator and as a parent, a child is totally unprepared to follow-up after your calm approach. They're ready for battle, and when you can't or won't give it to them, they secede. The power struggle is over.

Author James Baldwin writes, *"Children have never been very good at listening to their elders, but they have never failed to imitate them."* A power struggle can only continue if there are two people participating. Be smart by remaining calm and confident if even you have to fake it. Do not argue with children. As the adult, we must model the mature way to handle anger, disappointment, and frustration. Parents and teachers can grant legitimate power, offer choices and delegate responsibility where appropriate. Find out what children can be in charge of at home and in the classroom. These responsibilities should grow as a child grows. If a child has legitimate power in the classroom or home, fewer power struggles exist. This can be accomplished without compromising the authority of the adults or the self-esteem of the child.

CHAPTER 6

Tackling the Homework

Teaching children how to learn is just as important as teaching them what to learn.

A child comes home with an assignment. They tell the parent about the assignment, for example, multiplying unlike fractions and the parent volunteers to help. Once the parent looks at the problem, it's almost like reading something in another language, so they retreat and encourage the student to try to master it on his or her own. The student, tired from a long day at school, confused by the homework assignment, and frustrated with the lack of support, puts down his or her pencil and bows out from doing the homework. The outcome? Everyone loses.

Homework is a pain point for everyone—the parent, the teacher, and especially the student. Some teachers have opted out of issuing homework either because (a) their class assignments are engrossing enough to forgo the added work, (b) the time it takes to go over homework assignments takes away from the current lesson plan, or (c) homework is a barrier to family time and extracurricular activities. When homework becomes a problem for everyone involved in the educational journey, how effective is it? Who benefits from it when the child is frustrated, the parent is confused, and the teacher is overworked?

In many schools or classrooms, however, homework is still a major part of class expectations and the learning process. There's nothing wrong with this approach, but everyone needs to be equally committed to getting the best results possible, or else it's a hassle more than it is a help. In other schools, teachers are eliminating homework unless students did not complete their classwork during the school day.

With the introduction of Common Core and accelerated curricula concepts, parents have begun to lose their footing in the homework hurdle. Some of the very concepts that they use every day, such as basic math and reading comprehension, have become perplexing and frustrating. Parents struggle to properly tutor and support their children during homework assignments without first getting tutored and supported themselves.

Parents often fear to share with their children their own lack of understanding about a homework assignment or project. As parents, however, we should lead by example and show children the proper strategies to use when seeking help. By doing this, parents are modeling what we teach and showing children which tools to use when seeking help.

One of the things that a parent can do when it comes to homework help is to make several attempts to solve the problem. This shows the student the importance of diligence and problem-solving skills. The student will begin to understand the importance of devising strategies, testing alternative methods, checking results, and revising their approach. Although the parent may never come up with the right method (although they have the right answer), this approach shows a variety of requisite skills it takes to solve a problem. When a student understands that it's acceptable not to get the answer correct on the first attempt as long as you keep working to eventually find the right answer, they're building a growth mindset and grit.

Another strategy parents can use to offer homework help is to ask the student to teach you what they know. By giving the student the opportunity to become the teacher, they learn how to explain themselves, simplify a complex concept, and display their level of understanding. This behavior leads to the student's increased confidence. Ask the child to explain what they understand about the concept. Perhaps through their explanation, you may be able to understand the concept enough to fill in the blanks where your child is missing information.

Next, parents can do as much as possible to improve their child's homework habits and study skills. Parents and teachers remind children to study, yet children must be taught how to study. Homework can be used to build academic and executive function skills. Executive function skills are practical skills, such as organization, time management, goal-directed persistence, and impulse control. For example, my son was frustrated when learning to write paragraphs. I reminded him that paragraphs are just sentences and he could write sentences very well. I gave him several index cards to write one sentence on each. We started with an introduction and ended with the conclusion. He was quickly able to see how creating a paragraph was little more than putting a few sentences together. To this day, he often uses Post-it® notes or index cards to break down what appears to be lengthy assignments. This strategy allows him to feel confident in his ability to complete the task.

In addition, my children use a Time Timer® to monitor at-home activities. This silent timer allows them to see a visual display of how much time is left before a task should be completed. Building organizational and executive function skills is just as important as helping them with the content of their homework. It is just as important for adults to teach skills such as organization and goal setting as it is to help children learn reading and math strategies. At home, homework time should be carved out and sacred. By creating a supportive and well-equipped study environment (with access to tools and resources, such as books, writing utensils, and computers) that's free from distractions, you're drastically improving the chance they'll focus on the homework and learn the content.

Finally, parents, teachers, and students must communicate about homework. Homework is a tool to increase a student's ability to quickly assess and solve problems with limited guidance. Parents should know whether the teacher would prefer to have the parent help with the homework or return the unfinished portion with which the child needed help to the following class. Teachers should use homework to strengthen or accelerate their students' skills. Encourage communication about homework through an online site where parents and students can access homework assignments or ask questions. Teachers and parents should discuss how much time students should spend completing their homework. Homework should be viewed by all as a method of improving student understanding of a concept, not as a method of torture.

CHAPTER 7

Making the Grade

If my future were determined just by my performance on a standardized test, I wouldn't be here. I guarantee you that.
-MICHELLE OBAMA

As both a teacher and a parent, I've come to learn that one of the hardest things for my children to do is show me their grades. Yikes! You should see the anxiety they feel when they know they haven't met my expectations. It's also quite comical to see the ways that they'll avoid the conversation or the "show and tell" experience of showing me their grades. Of course, when their grades are B's or better, there's no hesitancy to boast about report cards or assignments. If they have a C or worse, however, tears and excuses begin to flow through the house when report card time comes around.

Grades are a deciding factor and a bargaining point in the educational journey. As a deciding factor, grades determine whether a student passes or fails or shows mastery or struggle. As a bargaining point, grades are used to get rewards, or if necessary, issue ultimatums. Unfortunately, grading policies have gotten a bad reputation. In some schools, test and quizzes are worth up to 70-80% of a student's grade, while in other schools, classwork and homework are an equal level to tests and quizzes. Grades can make students feel like they're not performing well enough. It can make parents feel there's something wrong with their approach to their child's education. And it can make teachers feel like they have to measure every little point to determine whether or not the students understand what they're learning.

Ultimately, grades should tell us what a student knows and what skills have been mastered. Proper student behavior is critical and should be reflected on the report card, but should not distort the academic grade. Students may master the content and complete all academic tasks, but demonstrate less than positive behavior in school. Another student can demonstrate stellar manners and behavior in class, yet struggle on key concepts in the class. Separating the academic grades from the conduct grades holds students accountable for both. The problem with letter grades is that it affects the self-esteem of the student and may not reflect the amount of effort a child puts forth. These grades can make them feel like, no matter how hard they try, they're not doing well enough. This is especially true when it comes to students who hover around the "C" level throughout their educational journey. Although many countries do not use letter grades or a point-based system, the United States educational system places a lot of value on grades. Whether or not we agree with this approach, educators and parents can put things in place to make dealing with letter grades easier for everyone involved.

The first thing we need to do, especially as parents and teachers, is to implement an "A for effort" mentality. The truth is, not every child will be an A student and not every child who receives a C deserves it. So many factors go unaccounted for or unweighted when it comes to the grading system. Many students don't get the grades they deserve for things that have no point value assigned to them. For instance, no points are given for perseverance, improved study habits, engagement, tutoring, asking questions, or staying late to finish assignments. Those are the things that show how much students may be trying to improve their grades, even if in the end, their grades don't reflect it. This effort alone showcases the student's smart decisions to do the work and ultimately, do well at it.

Because grading systems don't allow us to add points for all of the details of the learning experience, it's important that we applaud students for what they've done to show that they're trying to improve their performance. It can be disheartening to see that they've taken all of the necessary precautions to get the best grade possible but fallen short of the victory. Can you imagine how they feel? As parents and teachers, we have to remember that their egos are attached to those grades. So, when they've done anything significant toward getting better results and they miss the mark, a piece of their confidence crumbles, too.

"If my future were determined just by my performance on a standardized test, I wouldn't be here. I guarantee you that." This comment by former First Lady Michelle Obama reminds us that some students don't perform well on traditional tests. Tests—for anyone, children or adults—can create much anxiety, especially when they measure how good you are at something or how well

43

you understand it. The education system, however, tends to use tests and their results as one of the major indicators of how well a student understands a concept. In addition to being anxious, students are tasked with dealing with timeframes, distractions, and background issues—all while being expected to perform at their best. On top of that, the students know that whether they pass or fail a class or even a whole grade level often is heavily dependent on their test results. The pressure is unreal.

Unfortunately, we can't do much about tests, grading systems, point values, and any other metric used to evaluate a student's mastery of a concept. However, this challenges us to instill a "can do" attitude in students and encourage them to face their anxieties.

As a teacher, I've had plenty of students who came to school with winning personalities, great manners, all the right school supplies, attentiveness in class, and the willingness to collaborate with others or makeup work. These very same students have received a C on everything they've turned in. This also means that they've never been called onto the stage to receive a certificate for the honor roll or experienced celebrations for stellar performances. They've always been looked at as mid-performing students with room for improvement. It's crushing to see that they've worked so hard, yet it's not demonstrated in the grade book.

Parents must support a child's learning and performance. This means trying to understand letter grades as more than proof of mastery and asking questions about what he or she is learning outside of tests, assignments, and projects as well as evaluating any challenges and anxieties that exist. Most importantly, celebrate their efforts. Find appropriate ways to incorporate positive talk and praise to keep them motivated. Discuss the strategies that they are using to study and review material. Praise them for their effort, hard work, and perseverance. Research has demonstrated that this type of communication helps to promote a growth mindset in children. A growth mindset empowers children to continue to improve and understand that smart is not something that you just are, but something you become with continued hard work, correct strategy and effort. Parents and teachers must reinforce this growth mindset and remind our children they have the power to grow their intelligence.

It's true; as parents, we have high expectations for our children. We expect them to do their best, steadily improve, focus, and prove to us that they're trying to do right. Our job is to look beyond the letter grade and engage them in a discussion on their next set of learning goals. In guiding this discussion, find a balance between pushing children to do better and accepting their best efforts. Until you can find that balance, celebrate their work as a part of their journey. If the school overlooks their efforts during special programs and ceremonies, celebrate your child's accomplishments in your own way. Small things like a card, cake, and ice cream; a special outing; or an "I'm so proud of you" statement will show your child that although the school hasn't recognized his or her hard work, you, their parent, have. Interestingly enough, this may push them to do better more than any lecture or ultimatum could.

No matter if the student is an over-achiever who has become underwhelmed by their work or an under-performing student who has become overwhelmed by it, it's important that everyone involved in the educational journey begins to look at things beneath the surface of grades, and converses and celebrates these students' ability to bounce back, persevere and willingness to go the extra mile—not only how high they can measure on a grading system or how many certificates they can attain at an awards ceremony.

CHAPTER 8

Time for a Conference

Make no mistake about it: Next to parents and families, our teachers are the most important influence in our children's lives.

- KENNY GUINN

By midyear, most schools have scheduled at least one parent-teacher conference day. This time is set aside to allow parents and teachers (with or without the child) to discuss the student's progress thus far in the year. As educators and parents, we should come together to build on our connection with each other and our commitment to the child's success. This partnership should be built on our mutual respect for the influential roles that we play in the student's life and the shared aspiration to see the child reach their full academic potential.

When we acknowledge that we have a joint responsibility in supporting the student's success, parents become more proactive about motivating their child to reach academic goals, while teachers do their part by reaching out to the families to involve them in the progress. Because of this, parent–teacher conferences are an anticipated event for both parents and teachers.

Most of us probably can remember as children the butterflies we had in our stomachs when our parents and teachers connected. Knowing that adults were discussing our performance in class made us feel like a defendant waiting to hear a judge's verdict. Questions like, "Will they say that I work hard, or will they say I talk too much in class?" circled through our heads. Even for students who perform well, this time can be tense and frightening.

As grown-ups, we are also quite anxious about what will transpire during this short period of time. As teachers, we are nervous about the parents' views of our ability to properly instruct their children. And as parents, we are concerned about what will be said about our child and how it reflects on our parenting. Given all the nerves and anxiety mixed with this anticipation, it is expected and advisable for both parents and teachers to prepare for this day.

As parents, we try our very best to be involved in everything our children do. Unfortunately, the reality of life keeps us from covering every angle. So as not to be caught off-guard, it is smart for us to talk with our child before the big day. Ask them what they like most about school. What areas do they hope to improve in? Are there subjects that they particularly love? How do they feel about their classmates? Are there any issues you should know about? Although it is not necessary to come to the parent-teacher conference with a physical list of questions prepared, it certainly doesn't hurt, especially if you have a lot of concerns and don't want to risk forgetting one. You may want to consider asking the following questions: "What are my child's weakest and strongest subjects?" "Does my child engage in classroom discussions and participate in activities?" or "How can I help support my child's academic progress?"

All your preparation will be for nothing if you don't actually show up or if you arrive so late that there is barely enough time left to have a proper discussion. Teachers are often on an extremely tight schedule and a 10-minute late arrival can have a major impact on how much time they will have with you. Be ready and present that day, and ensure that you've made prior arrangements at home or work to ensure that you arrive on time.

As the educator and the one initiating the conference, it is your responsibility to prepare by sending out invitations, reviewing the student's work, creating an agenda on the key issues to be discussed, and ensuring that the parents feel welcomed when they arrive. Thanks to modern technology, there is a plethora of ways to disseminate information about the upcoming parent-teacher conference to our student's families. We can e-mail invitations or post the event on the school web page or social media. We can even send a text message or send a note home with the child.

Teachers should try to schedule conferences with all of your students' parents. All parents should know how their child is progressing regardless of whether their child is excelling or is struggling. Family dynamics, such as blended families or divorce, may make scheduling more than one conference necessary. Try to accommodate the parents by allowing for phone conferences or web-based meetings. This will allow all of the grown-ups to participate and be informed about the child's progress. Be prepared to gather all their graded assignments and assessments to create a portfolio of the child's schoolwork that you can present to the parent. Include time for the parents to ask questions to avoid presenting a one-way mode of communication. Student-led conferences are often appropriate and beneficial. The student understands that the adults in his or her life share a common goal of his or her success. Students may share work samples and articulate what they have learned thus far in the year. An action plan should be discussed in the last few minutes of the conference that can outline how to help their child move forward academically. Get a verbal agreement from the parent that they will play their part in helping the child reach their academic goals.

The parents you are about to meet are probably pretty nervous. Welcome the parents into a warm and friendly environment by preparing the classroom with comfortable chairs for adults. It would be advisable not to have a desk separating you to avoid giving off that principal versus the problem child vibe. Some teachers go to the extent of setting out water, light snacks, or even a bowl of candy. The goal is to minimize nervousness and to create an atmosphere of cooperation and open communication. The parent-teacher conference is our opportunity to walk parents through what child has accomplished thus far in the school year.

Parent-teacher conferences should only be one of many communications that occur between teachers and parents throughout the academic school year. Both the parent and teacher have learned something valuable about the student during the initial meeting. No matter the format of the conference, the teacher now has a better understanding of the student's home life, motivations, and personal obstacles, if any, and the parent has gained insight into how their child behaves in the school setting and under the guidance of another influential figure. Ultimately, the child knows that the grown-ups are working together to support his or her academic success.

CHAPTER 9

Handling Spring Fever

You're not obligated to win. You're obligated to
keep trying to do the best you can every day.
-MARIAN WRIGHT EDELMAN

Spring is the start of rejuvenation. The days are longer. The weather is better. Everything comes to life. Spring makes everyone want to explore, get moving, and enjoy the day. This is especially true for teachers and students, who, unfortunately, still are in the classroom for six or more hours a day—longing to break free and get the school year over with.

The spring season is challenging for students. Everything seems to point in the direction of "go outside, yell, play, and feel free." Meanwhile, as teachers and parents, we're still urging our children to stay focused, limit playtime, and finish the school year strong. By the spring season, everyone is tired and running the last leg of the end-of-school race. Some of us continue to push through the race with the same energy and passion as we started, and some of us have fizzled out and are willing to settle with whatever position of the race we end up.

To finish strong, we must remember how much we've contributed to this journey. Everyone involved in the school year—students, teachers, and parents—have contributed so much effort and made so many sacrifices to get to this point that it would be foolish to give it all up now. It would be reckless to abandon the long hours on homework and projects or the weekly quizzes and assessments for the desire to relax in the sun all day. It would be pointless to have endured this much work to simply walk away with a "let's just get this over with" attitude.

Spring is the time to rejuvenate. It's not the time to slow down and jeopardize everything you've worked for—whether you are the student, parent, or the teacher. Instead, spring is the time to kick things up a notch and make up for any inconsistencies, slow starts, or learning curves. If we think of spring as the time of year that we can revitalize energy then this will help us move forward during this often-challenging time of the school year.

The school year is really at its peak season during the spring. Just about everyone is getting prepared to engage in state or district assessments that help to determine whether or not the students have achieved a certain level of academic growth. We're ready to measure how much they've learned since the previous year's assessments. We're ready to evaluate their working knowledge and the skills that they've developed. And, yes, just like the students, we're also ready for school to be over with.

To make it through the final leg of the race toward the end of the school year, we have to mentally and emotionally train ourselves and our children to win that race. Any great athlete knows that training and preparation are vital to winning a race. They know that finishing the race strong is just as meaningful as finishing the race in first place.

To prepare our mindset for completing the school year with just as much fervor and perseverance (if not more) as when we started, it's important to begin the school year by setting goals and establishing commitments. Goals and commitments create accountability, which serves as a system of checks and balances that aim toward getting the job done.

As adults, if we create these school-year goals and commitments, we are holding ourselves accountable to taking every measure to see to it that our jobs are done as expected. If we want structured and organized lessons, then we're holding ourselves accountable to creating and maintaining environments that are conducive to these sessions. If we want every assignment completed and submitted on time, then we hold ourselves accountable for grading papers and providing prompt and effective feedback. If we want children to finish the school year with a wealth of new learning, then we're holding ourselves accountable for creating engaging lessons, attending conferences, and adjusting our instruction to meet their learning needs. If we want our children to be successful throughout the whole school year, then even during the spring, when we're tired and begging for the stress of the school year to be over with, we're holding ourselves accountable to staying focused until it's actually over.

Now, with children, we first have to help them understand the value of goal setting and commitments. This is difficult if our children are not yet mature enough to understand what these words really mean and how they affect their progress and growth.

So, we should talk to them about focusing and finishing what they've started.

Children can become easily distracted and discouraged. One day they're totally committed and excited about the possibilities or an assignment. And the next day, after the weight of the responsibility and workload has settled in, they're discouraged and disinterested. Our discussions with them should be geared toward the following: "You've worked hard this far, continuing the same effort will pay off in the end." This works on every level from prekindergarten and learning how to write their names or color in the lines to high school and taking the SATs and finals.

The keys to finishing strong that work inside the classroom and at home—even after spring break and the first taste of freedom that the spring season offers—are motivation, accountability, and perseverance. It's up to parents and teachers to encourage and remind ourselves to show up and be present in school and at home and to help our children to focus and commit to finishing this lap of their educational journey.

CHAPTER 10

Keeping Stress in Check

Everybody thinks you should be happy just because you're
young. They don't see the wars that we fight every single day
- THE FREEDOM WRITERS

What could be more stressful than being an adult with bills, a job, a household to run, children to raise, and trying to maintain some sort of sanity in today's busy world? Being a teenager! As an adult, we often remind children to enjoy their childhood while they can or emphasize how little they actually have to deal with on a regular basis. But, what if we're actually very wrong about how much children, especially teens, have to deal with?

According to the results of the Stress in America Survey released by the American Psychological Association, **http:// www.apa.org/news/press/releases/2014/02/teen-stress.aspx** teens report higher levels of stress than adults during the school year. Stress is even higher for students living in at-risk situations according to Dr. Frank Kros, president of The Upside Down

Organization and Executive Vice President of The Children's Guild. He states, "Traumatic stress is the biggest unseen obstacle to healthy development and robust learning for at-risk children and youth." Although we may think that children should not have anything to be stressed about, the weight of this information should be taken extremely seriously. If our children are in school for nine months out of the year (and some are even in school year-round), does this mean that they spend a good portion of their pre-adult lives dealing with stress? Probably. As adults, we know how much stress can alter our moods and performances, but how often do we take into consideration the amount of stress and pressure our children are facing each day in school.

Stress is our body's natural response to adverse situations. We try to balance the pressure for students to perform with the motivation and incentives that make them want to work as hard as they can. But really, how often does that work for us? Adults have an incredible amount of pressure placed on their shoulders on a regular basis. Some of us handle it very well because of high levels of maturity, mental and emotional stamina, or the desire not to let the world swallow us up and spit us out. For children, however, who have not yet received mental clarity, maturity, self-motivation practices, and fortitude, they just feel a lot of pressure to do a lot of things they don't want to do or don't know how to do—and get stellar results from it—especially when it comes to school.

Although we can't eliminate all stress for our children, we can teach them strategies on how to cope with stress when it occurs. In fact, at the same time we issue roles, responsibilities, expectations, and demands, we also should be issuing self-care methods, decompression ideas, and coping strategies. It's only fair.

When you fly on an airplane, the flight attendant instructs you to put on your oxygen mask, before helping others. Why is this an important rule for ensuring survival? Because if you run out of oxygen, you can't help anyone else. This metaphor is true for those of us who parent or teach children. For us to equip our children with proper self-care and calming strategies, it's imperative that we start with ourselves. Starting with ourselves not only gives children something to model themselves after but also helps us to maintain our momentum as we balance our busy lives and demands with theirs.

When it comes to dealing with the demands of our children's education, whether we are their teachers or their parents, we should approach stressful and challenging situations with mindful breaths, optimism, and positive talk. Sure, it may sound like it's easier said than done, but they actually are just practiced strategies that eventually become habit.

The words that we use with children really matter. And whether or not we know it, the words we say can either add to their stress level or minimize it. Our words can dictate how much more willing a child is to succeed and how much more likely they are to stop trying. As adults, if we learn how to craft our statements so that they make children want to try, they will feel more comfortable asking questions and stating their insecurities. Positive talk is not simply about being cheerful and approachable, it's about motivating a child to examine their strategies, put forth their best effort, and persevere. However, there are two sides to this "positive talk" coin. We must learn how to use this tool to benefit our children's situations and to benefit our own.

Sometimes the parental position in a child's journey can be

just as demanding and stressful as the child's position. We have to be willing to sit down and do homework with them when a million other things are going on. We have to show up to PTA meetings, conferences, and important events, although we're expected to show up at work or to own appointments, which always seem to conflict. We have to work late on school assignments and projects alongside our children as if we are the ones trying to earn an A. We have to be in school mentally, although we're not in school physically, meaning that we have to be ready to meet the demands of the classroom and the school—even when we're not the student. We have to be ready to listen when they have fights with their best friend, are embarrassed from a fall in the cafeteria or don't make the second round of tryouts on the soccer team. These situations not only become stressful, but also breed stressful responses, which our children pick up on, mimic, and absorb.

The next time you find yourself having to help your child with a challenging homework assignment, try to approach it in a calm and confident manner to minimize both of your stress levels. If the child expresses frustration by saying "This is hard, I can't do it", respond with a calm affirming statement such as "You're right. This looks a little hard, and you may not be able to do it yet. Let's work together to see how we can get through this." Essentially, remove you and your child from the immediate pressure of having to solve the problem and instead position yourself in a calm and neutral environment. Use some positive talk such as "I remember when you struggled with your 7 times tables and now you're a wiz at those" before discussing the challenges of the problem. Discuss your knowledge (or lack thereof) on the topic. Allow your child to teach you what they know and for you to do the same. Basically, to create the optimal learning environment, you actually have to try to minimize the stress of the situation and reduce your personal stress and frustration as well. By doing this, you're teaching your child how to cope with a situation, communicate concerns, regroup, and then feel empowered to handle the task before them. The beautiful part of this strategy is that it works with education and it works with life.

We also should realize that sometimes helping our children manage their stress levels involves understanding that they don't have the maturity to respond to stress in the same ways that we do—because they're children. This often means that we must educate them about the best ways to handle the stressful situations that may occur at school.

As a parent, it's really important for us to recognize situations that bring stress to their lives and use them as teachable moments but also use them as moments to stand in for them and show how much we're willing to advocate for them. This means having regular conversations with the teachers, writing the notes to request extra time on assignments when they've been sick, and looking over the details before our children turn in their work. Those moments, which are highly stressful for students are moments when we can say, "Relax, I've got your back."

When teachers are feeling overwhelmed, they may not be the only ones paying the price. Students' stress levels are being elevated as a result of their teacher's exhaustion, and often vice versa. This may not come as a major surprise, but a study from the University of British Columbia (UBC), students-and-teachers/is the first that has established a strong link—a "stress contagion"—between a teacher's occupational stress and a student's physiological strain. http://news.ubc.ca/2016/06/27/ubc-study-finds-stress-contagio n-amongst-students-and-teachers/

What does all of this mean? When teachers are stressed from their work, it passes on to the students, and in turn, they become stressed about their work. In no way does this create a support- ive and conducive learning environment. No one can win in this situation.

As teachers, it's important to use your classroom as a safe space for both you and your students. We know that sometimes school is the only place where a child receives a meal, a greeting, or a hug. Thus, it is our responsibility to also make it a place where a child feels like they can reach their full potential and escape from the external stressors and grievances of the outside world. Morning meetings, predictable routines and positive relation- ships help schools to be engaging and inspiring and not overly stressful and draining for the teacher or the student.

Help your students and children identify their emotions con- cerning the things that are causing them stress. Whether it's an- gry about being bullied or hurt from feeling left out, identifying these feelings and stressors is important. Don't tell children how they *should* feel because then you're undermining their feelings and creating an additional stressful situation in which they feel that they don't have a voice. Listen to them and try to hear and understand why they are feeling a certain way. It is easy for an adult with a fully developed prefrontal cortex to say, "don't let what your friends think of you bother you" or "ignore the kids who are laughing at you." This kind of "reinforcement" is contrary to the developmental stage of children who are sensitive and want to fit in with their peers. Often, what a child's peers think is more important than what parents or teachers think.

Strategies such as mindful breathing, meditation, prayer, and positive self-talk can effectively help children handle stress inside the classroom and at home, often without the help of an adult. Also, be sure to teach children when to seek help from an adult. Parents and teachers also have to be aware of when children may need additional support. Some feelings of anxiety and depression occur in most children and adults, but long-term periods of either may require consultation with a mental health professional.

Childhood stress can have a variety of triggers, and it can sneak up on kids. Open and honest communication about feelings and emotions reminds kids they can seek help when life feels complicated, but the most valuable gift you can give children is unconditional love. Kids will encounter stress and hard days— that's part of life. Knowing that adults in their lives will listen and care about them empowers them to work through their feelings and move forward.

CHAPTER 11

Finishing Strong

The object of teaching a child is to enable
him to get along without the teacher.

– ELBERT HUBBART

Finally! It's June and the end of the school year. It feels like you've been holding your breath all year and now, after about eight months of structured chaos, you can exhale. Or can you? Although we've started to unwind, dismantle classrooms, put away leftover school supplies, and think about the long-awaited summer vacation, technically, school isn't over.

During the final weeks before the end of the school year, we should take some time to reflect on this educational journey. At this point, what's done is done when it comes to grades and lesson plans, but that doesn't mean that we should call it quits with our goal of instilling the power and importance of education into our children. Teachers may want to use this time to reinforce all of the lessons they've taught throughout the past nine months.

Parents may want to review the learning successes and struggles that have occurred throughout the year. What's even more substantial than all of these last-minute measures is celebrating the academic and social growth of our children.

When a child approaches the classroom during the fall, they're full of apprehension and curiosity along with a bit of insecurity. They have tons of potential that needs to be uncovered, explored, and nurtured for them to achieve all of their academic and social goals. So, as a team, parents, teachers, and administrators commit to helping children reach the full extent of their academic powers and make a promise to encourage a healthy social life. Therefore, at the end of the school year, no matter their shortcomings, pitfalls, detours, or moments of doubt, each child should be celebrated.

Education doesn't take breaks. The ever-growing process of learning, brain stimulation, and skill development doesn't pause because school bells have stopped ringing. In fact, when we close down the classrooms over the summer, it's actually the perfect time to increase our learning in new directions and with new methods. The end of the school year is not the end of learning. It's just a change in the methods in which we teach and learn.

Nearly all children suffer from gaps in their learning progress when they don't actively engage in educational activities during the summer. This is known as the "summer slide" in the educational setting. This slide can put children two to three months behind on their progress, which means by the time they return to school in the fall, most of what they retained during the previous school year has significantly diminished. It makes you think: If we spend nine months of a year in school, yet lose three months of education from summer break, we only retain six months' worth of education every school year. How far behind are our children falling when we don't maintain their education throughout the summer?

Sure, the days of waking early, boarding school buses, and sitting in the classroom fade as the summer break makes an appearance. Gone are the homework assignments, projects, and benchmark tests for students. The lesson planning, grading, and hours of teaching groups of children are memories. And for parents, the constant struggle of getting your children to stay focused on their schoolwork temporarily ceases. However, summer break is just as much a critical part of the learning experience as the rest of the school year.

At the end of the school year, the children who have demonstrated stellar growth and met every benchmark are applauded and received with enthusiasm and glimmering hope. These students, however, were not the only students in the classroom. Other students gave it their best shots and came up shy of receiving honor roll. Some students struggled with their daily attendance requirements because they lacked motivation or faced circumstances beyond their control, so they missed the mark for perfect attendance, yet they showed up regardless of their feelings or situations. Yet other students couldn't break the C barrier, but pulled from the rear and removed the D grades from their records. Some children were happy and jubilant about being in school, but it didn't show in their schoolwork because of their academic challenges or underdeveloped passion for learning. Every child will not be the "perfect student," which may be hard to define anyway, but nonetheless, every student should be celebrated.

CONCLUSION

"There are only two lasting bequests we can hope to give our children. One of these is roots, the other, wings."
-JOHANN WOLFGANG VON GOETHE

We want children to be smart, courageous, and respectful. We teach them to set goals. We do our best to protect them from the dangers of the world. We watch who they associate with and introduce them to things that'll help them grow. From the moment we learn we are becoming parents or guardians, we begin to do everything that we can to get smart and give our children the best opportunities to lead happy and successful lives.

And although we do all of these things—not to mention attend to surprises like urgent care visits, lost library books or broken eyeglasses—we still have to do more. This is especially true when it comes to teaching our children about being independent, making the right decisions and getting back on track when they've made bad choices.

It's easy to say we want the best for our children. After all, why would we want anything else? But wanting the best for them and even attempting to give them the best, becomes most effective when we teach them to want the best for *themselves*. From the early moments when we were teaching them how to walk, we held their hands and cushioned the falls until it was time for them to take their first steps on their own. We watched, anxiously, as they put one foot in front of the other and progressed toward a destination of their choice. We cheered them on when they made countless steps and we soothed them when they fell on their bottoms. Teachers and parents have different roles to play, yet both are coaches steering for the same outcome of success.

The point is, we taught and watched them, encouraged them to try it on their own, and loosened our grip to let them explore for themselves. We were still right there, acting as floor cushions to guard them when they stumbled or to help them up when they fell. In the same moments, we were trying to teach them independence; we also were creating support systems.

Teaching independence takes skill and tenacity. However, it also takes time. Childhood is something that should be treasured and nurtured. It shouldn't be rushed or looked at as something that should be "over with" by a certain age. If we have to hold our children's hands longer than other parents do, then so be it. If we have to reteach a concept for our students to understand it, then so be it. Parenting and teaching aren't about letting children go at a certain age. It's about letting them grow and pointing them in the right direction.

This couldn't be truer when it comes to education. Education is the key to helping our children to make smarter and more informed decisions. School is more than just reading and writing. School helps to shape their minds, teach them about accountability, and show them how to solve complex problems. The more time and care that we, their parents and teachers, invest into their education, the more well-rounded and well-prepared our children will become. Education is a springboard into the world, giving our children the requisite skills that it takes to navigate the world, make decisions about their paths, and, ultimately, succeed in what they do.

The Bible in Proverbs 22:6 gives us the best example of what effective parenting and teaching should look like: "Train up a child in the way he should go and when he is old he will not depart from it." This paramount teaching shows us how important it is to stand with our children, talk to them, and encourage them—showing them the right ways to grow and develop—so that when they become adults and encounter their own paths, they'll remember what they've been taught and, hopefully, take the right direction.

We should work to plant solid roots in children that spread to multiple areas of their lives, including relationships, athletics, spirituality, health and wellness, and more, to keep them grounded so they sprout and stand tall as they grow. Our role as teachers and parents are like gardeners. We plant seeds of knowledge and wisdom. We nurture them with hope and love. We prune the weeds of disappointment and hurt and expose them to healthy environments. We do all of this while constantly improving on our craft so that we become better while making them better.

As the school year ends, and children graduate or complete another grade in school, remember that this is neither the beginning nor the end of our job. It's not the sole responsibility of any one person (teacher, student, administrator, coach, or parent) to teach a child. Although at some times, it may feel like we're alone in the education process, we're not. And although we may feel like no one is paying attention to our efforts or acknowledging our strides, our children see us and we matter to them.

Childhood is a journey that goes from roots to wings. There's no defined process. There's no definite outcome. Each day should be taken one at a time. Each goal should be set and reached, one at a time. As parents and teachers commit to being school smart, the expectation is that every academic year is geared toward raising and developing capable, independent and happy children, then along with faith, hard work, and good times that overshadow the bad, children will grow wings that take them places beyond even their imagination.

SHAUNA F. KING, ED.S. is an

educational consultant who also serves as adjunct faculty for LaSalle University, a school climate coach with The University of Maryland Positive Schools Center and a certified presenter for The Upside Down Organization. She is a former principal and classroom teacher with over 20 years of experience in public and non-public school settings.

Shauna has a talent and passion for connecting with adults who have chosen to serve children. This passion has led to invitations to present nationally as well as internationally. A self-proclaimed "Yelling Teacher in Recovery," Shauna shares practical and research-based strategies to improve teacher, parent and student engagement.

Shauna holds a Bachelor's Degree from Morgan State University, a Master's degree in Education from Bowie State University and an Education Specialist degree in Adult Learning from Walden University. An active member of her church and community, Shauna is a proud wife and mother of two children, who are the joy of her life.

Connect with the Author www.shaunafking.com

Twitter@shaunafking

Email: shaunafking@gmail.com